RECORDED VERSIONS GUITAR

AUTHENTIC TRANSCRIPTIONS
WITH NOTES AND TABLATURE

THE RACONTEURS
Broken Boy Soldiers

Music transcriptions by Pete Billmann

ISBN-13: 978-1-4234-2314-0
ISBN-10: 1-4234-2314-3

HAL•LEONARD® CORPORATION

7777 W. BLUEMOUND RD. P.O. BOX 13819 MILWAUKEE, WI 53213

Visit Hal Leonard Online at
www.halleonard.com

Steady, as She Goes

Words and Music by Brendan Benson and Jack White

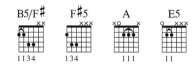

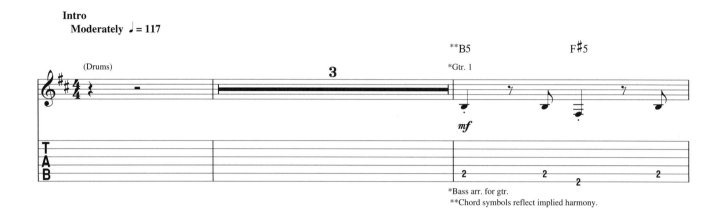

*Bass arr. for gtr.
**Chord symbols reflect implied harmony.

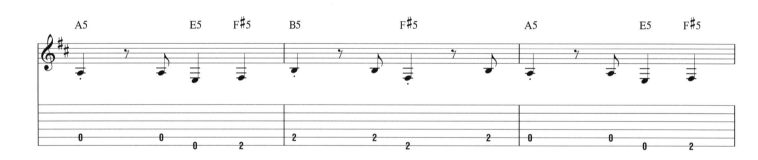

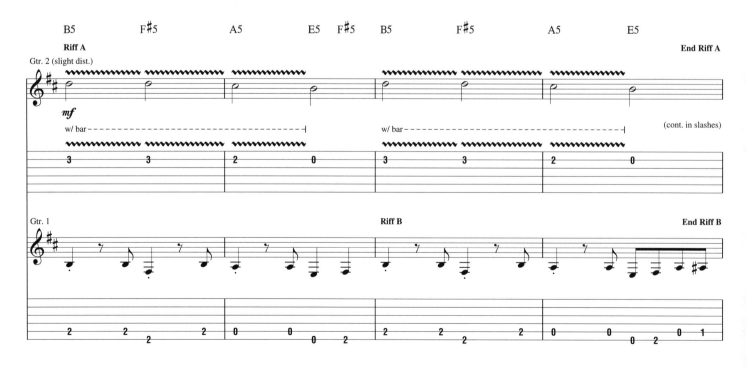

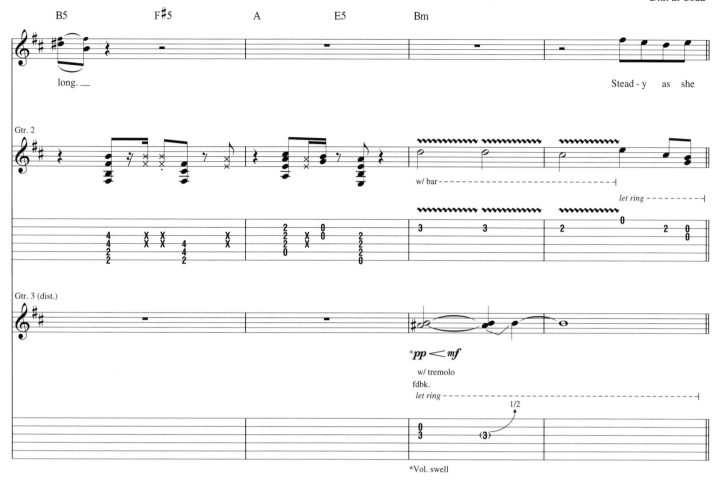

⊕ Coda
Refrain

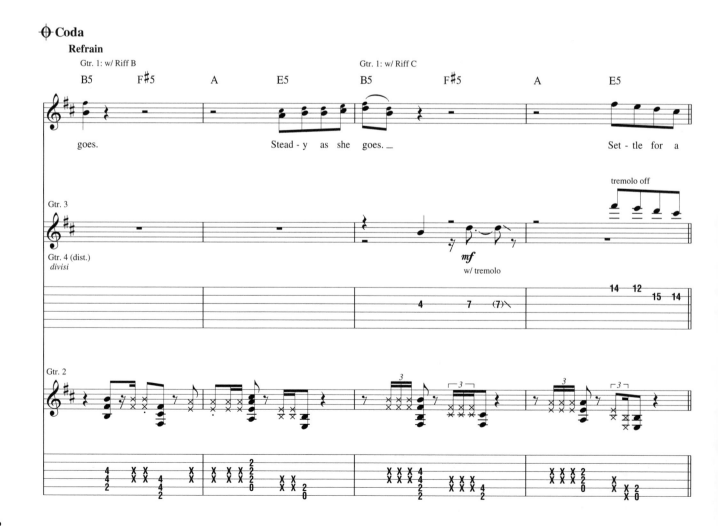

Bridge

Gtr. 1: w/ Riff B
Gtr. 2: w/ Rhy. Fig. 3 (2 times)

Gtr. 1: w/ Riff C

world _ nei - ther up or down. _____ Sell it to the crowd _ now that's gath - ered 'round. _____

(Set - tle for a world _ nei - ther up or down. Sell it to the crowd _ that is

Gtr. 3

Gtr. 4
divisi

tremolo off   *let ring - - - -*

Gtr. 5 (dist.)

mf

Gtr. 1: w/ Riff B (2 times)

_____ Set - tle for a girl _ nei - ther up or down. _____ Sell it to the

gath - ered 'round.   Set - tle for a girl _ nei - ther up or down.

let ring - - - -   *let ring - - - -*

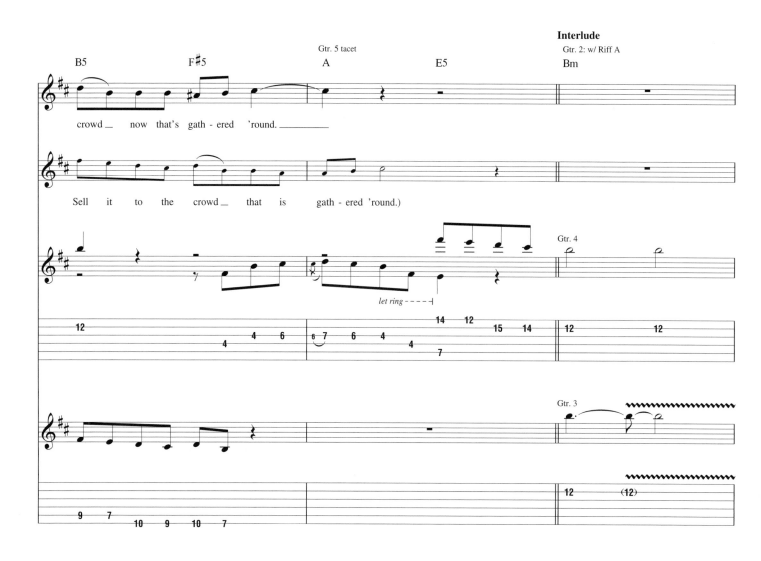

B5   F#5   Gtr. 5 tacet   A   E5   Bm

crowd ___ now that's gath - ered 'round. _____

Sell it to the crowd ___ that is gath - ered 'round.)

Gtr. 4

let ring - - - - -

Gtr. 3

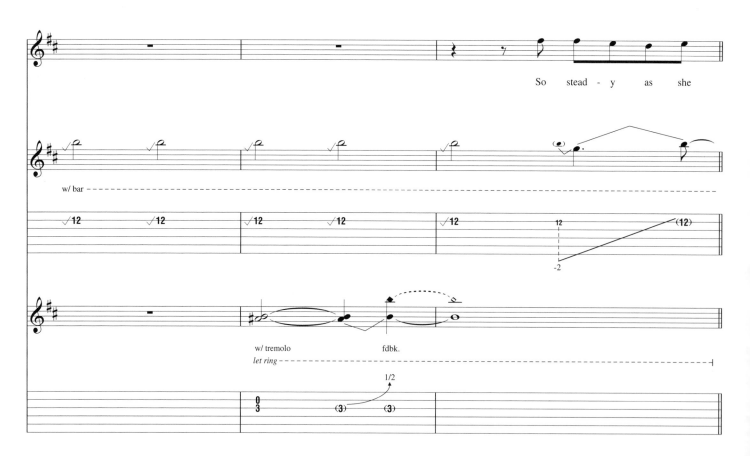

So stead - y as she

w/ bar -

w/ tremolo   fdbk.

let ring -

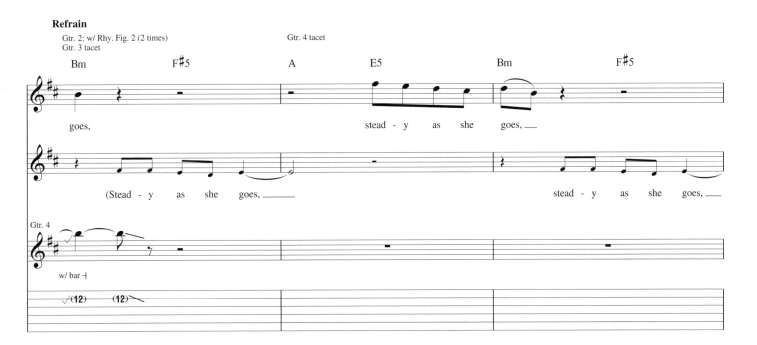

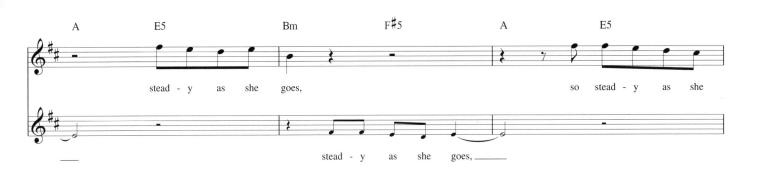

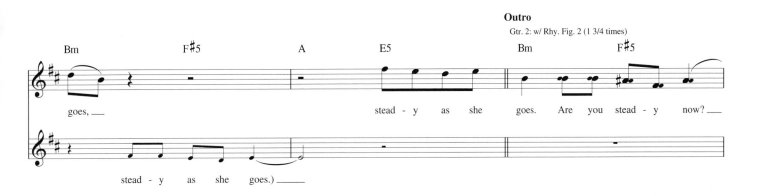

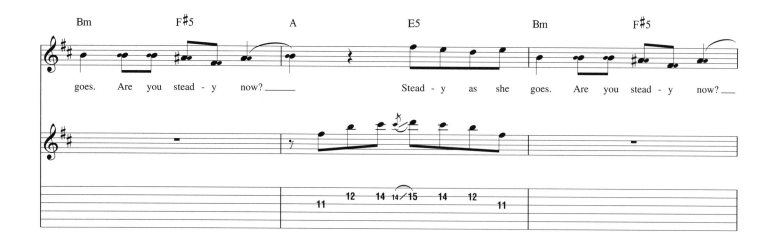

Bm   F#5   A   E5   Bm   F#5

goes. Are you stead - y now? _____   Stead - y as she goes. Are you stead - y now?___

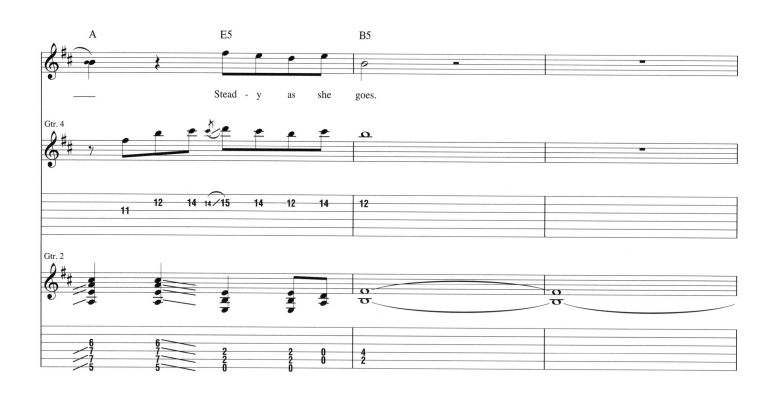

A   E5   B5

___   Stead - y as she goes.

Gtr. 4

Gtr. 2

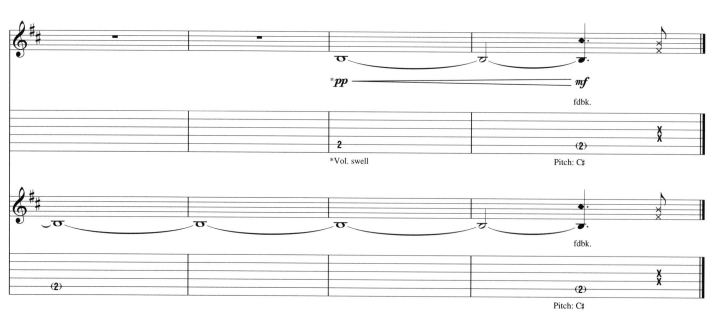

*pp ———————————————————— mf

fdbk.

*Vol. swell   Pitch: C#

fdbk.

Pitch: C#

Hands

Words and Music by Brendan Benson and Jack White

Intro
Free time

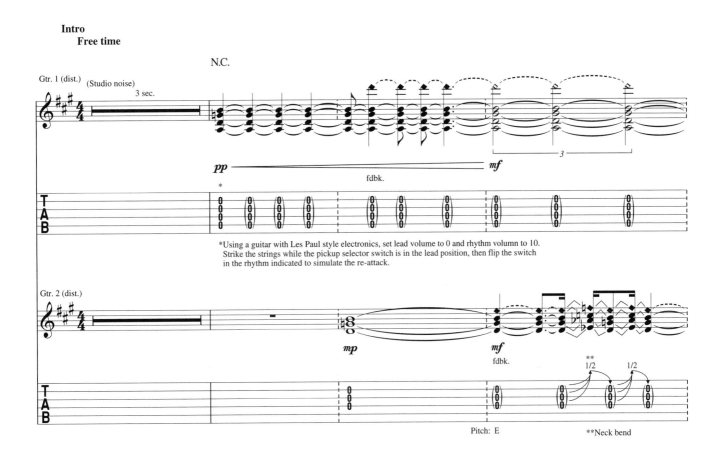

*Using a guitar with Les Paul style electronics, set lead volume to 0 and rhythm volumn to 10.
Strike the strings while the pickup selector switch is in the lead position, then flip the switch
in the rhythm indicated to simulate the re-attack.

Pitch: E

**Neck bend

Moderately ♩ = 96

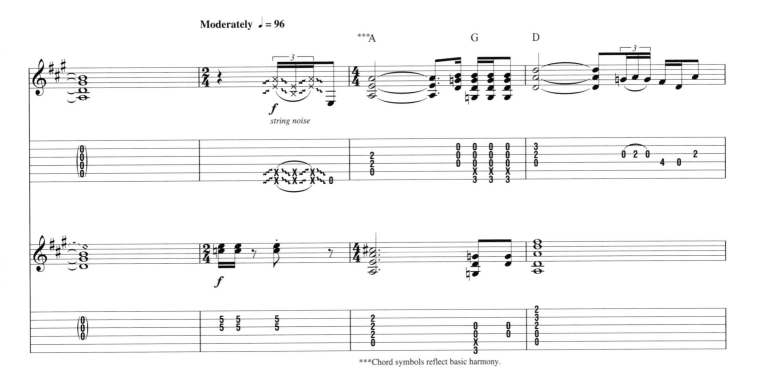

***Chord symbols reflect basic harmony.

Verse

1. Girl, you got those hands __ that heal, _____ help me get in

to me, it's a song and I know what to say.

End Rhy. Fig. 2

let ring

End Rhy. Fig. 2A

let ring

Interlude

*Neck bend

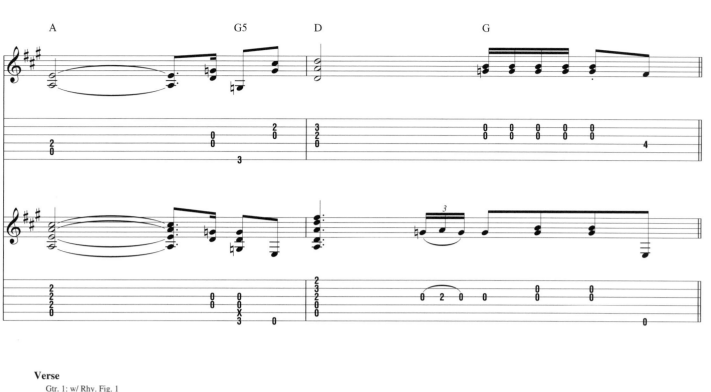

Verse

Gtr. 1: w/ Rhy. Fig. 1
Gtr. 2: w/ Rhy. Fill 1

2. Girl, you got those eyes ___ that see, ___ help me find the

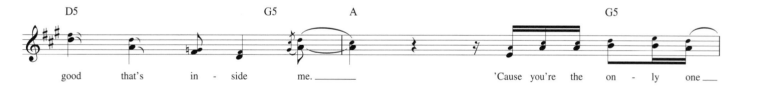

good that's in - side me. ___ 'Cause you're the on - ly one ___

___ who real - ly knows ___ how the feel - ing comes ___ and ___ why it ___ goes. ___

Chorus

Gtrs. 1 & 2: w/ Rhy. Figs. 2 & 2A

___ When you're with ___ me, there's ___ a light ___ and ___ I ___ can see ___

___ my ___ way. When you speak ___ to me, it's a song ___ and I know ___ what to ___

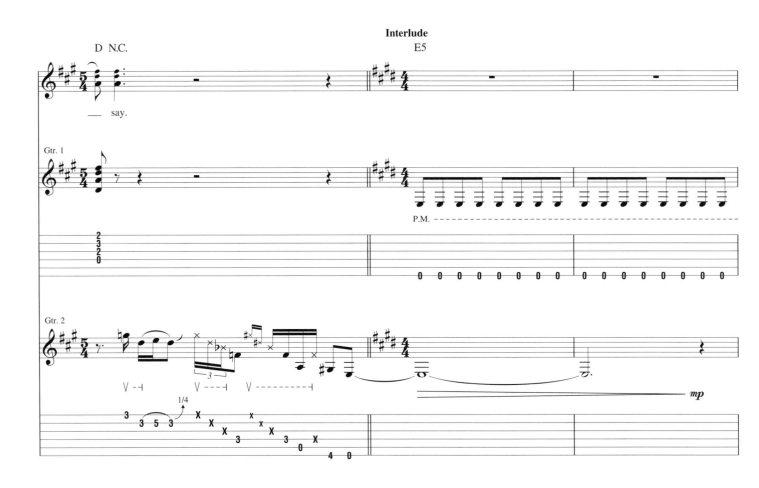

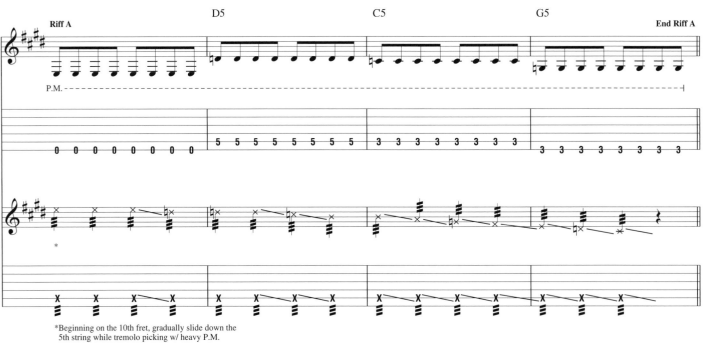

*Beginning on the 10th fret, gradually slide down the
5th string while tremolo picking w/ heavy P.M.

Bridge

Gtr. 1: w/ Riff A (2 times)
Gtr. 2 tacet

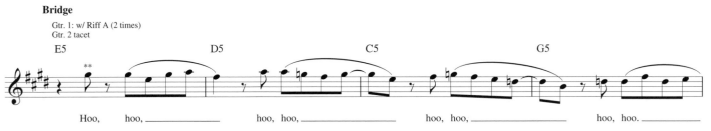

Hoo,   hoo, _____   hoo, hoo, _____   hoo, hoo, _____   hoo, hoo. _____

**Voc. doubled, next 12 meas.

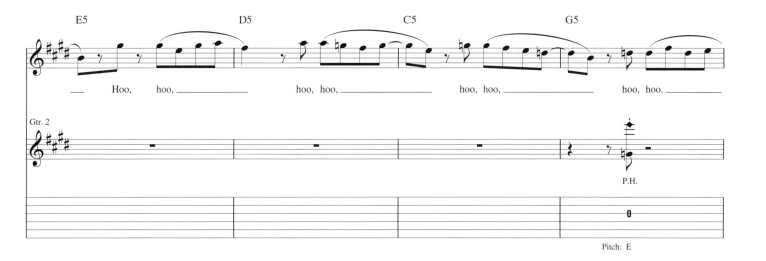

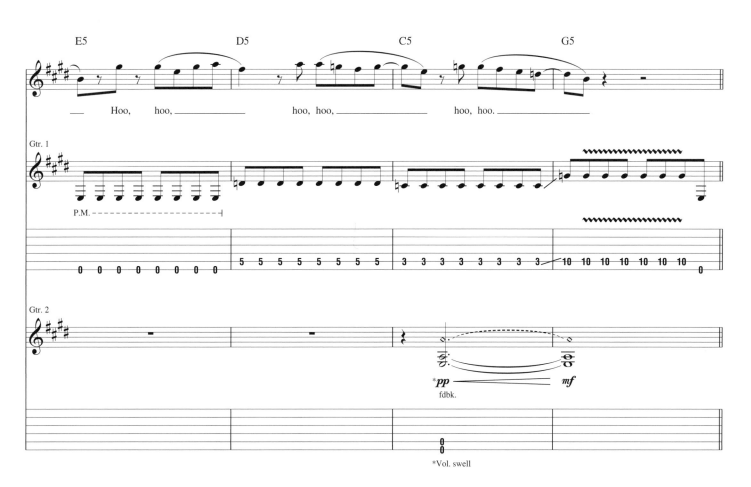

Outro-Chorus

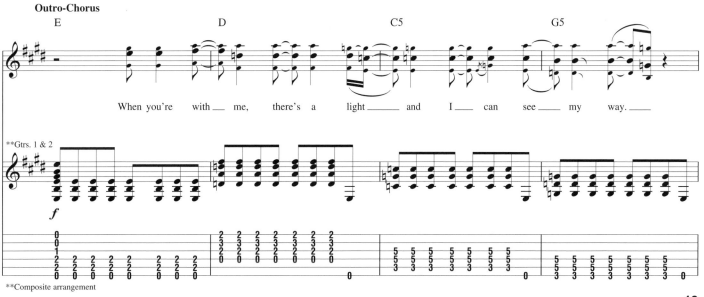

When you're with me, there's a light and I can see my way.

**Composite arrangement

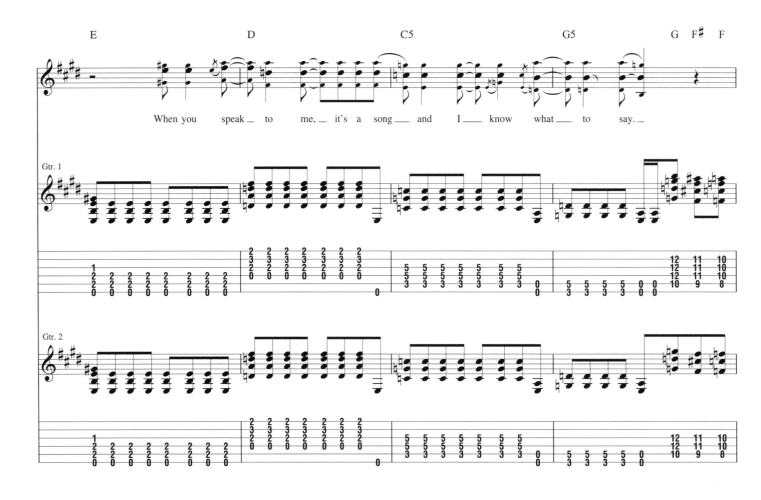

When you speak _ to _ me, _ it's a song _ and I _ know what _ to say. _

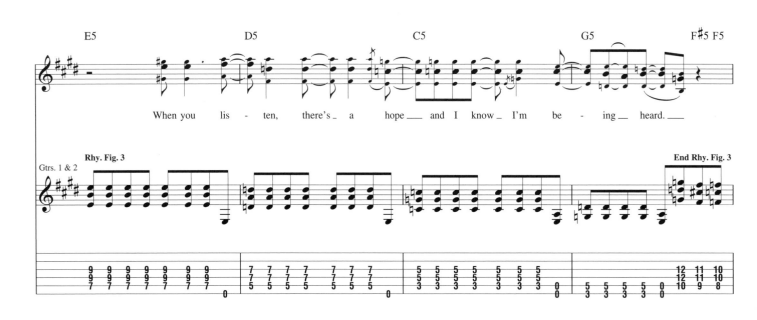

When you lis - ten, there's _ a hope _ and I know _ I'm be - ing _ heard. _

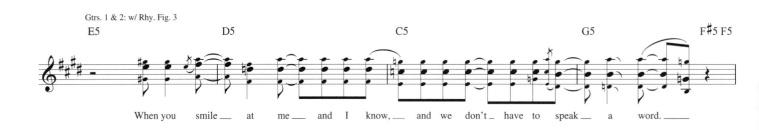

When you smile _ at me _ and I know, _ and we don't _ have to speak _ a word. _

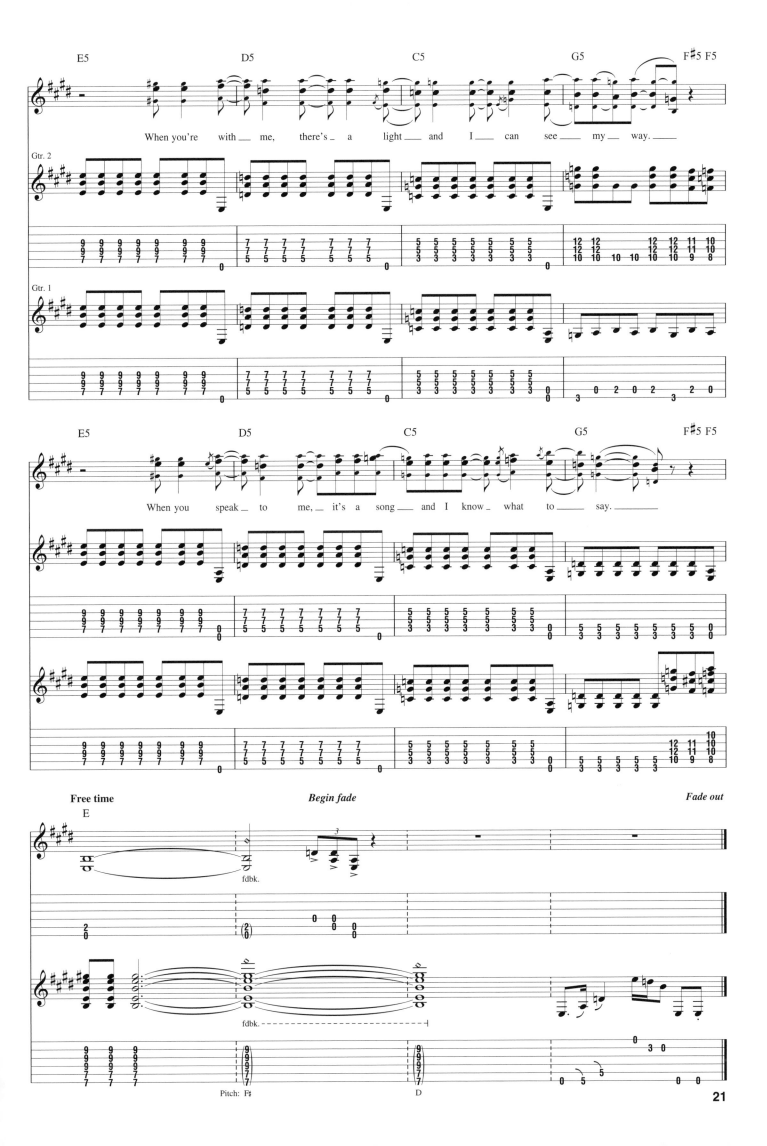

When you're with me, there's a light and I can see my way.

When you speak to me, it's a song and I know what to say.

Broken Boy Soldier

Words and Music by Brendan Benson and Jack White

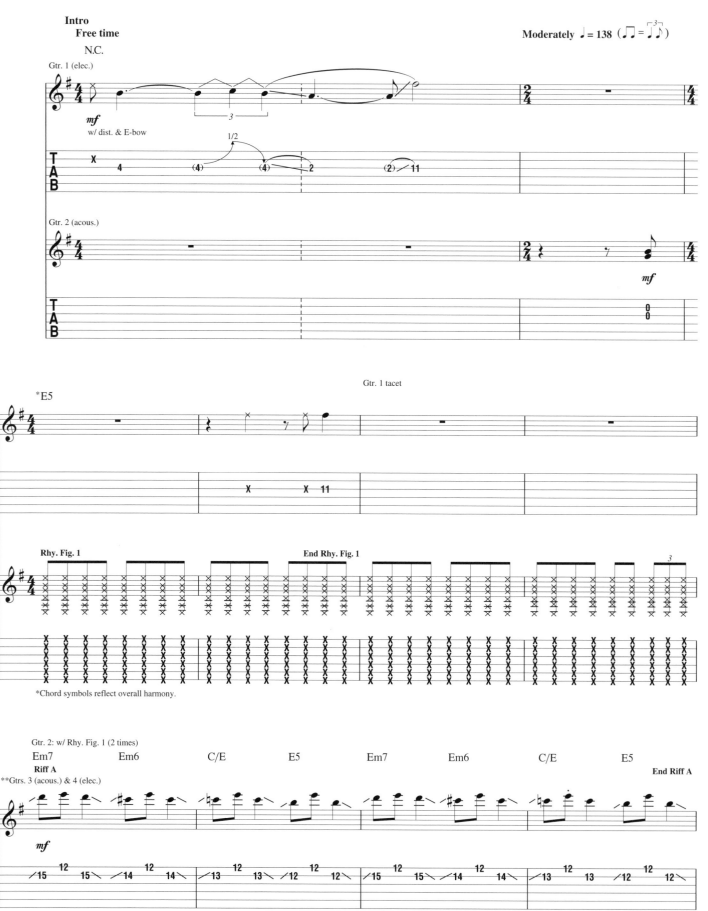

I ain't ask-in' no-bod-y but my-self, and I want you to know this.

Gtrs. 2 & 4: w/ Rhy. Fig. 2

E5   C5   B5   A5   G5

Gtrs. 2 & 4: w/ Riff B   Gtrs. 2 & 4: w/ Rhy. Fig. 2

Em   E5 C5   B5   A5   G5

And I want you to know this.

Verse

Gtrs. 2 & 4: w/ Riff B (8 times)

Em

2. You're rif - fling through a box of toys that were hand-ed down to me.

Riff C   **End Riff C**

fdbk.

Gtr. 1: w/ Riff D

Well, I'm child and man___ then child___ a - gain.___ The boy nev - er gets old - er.

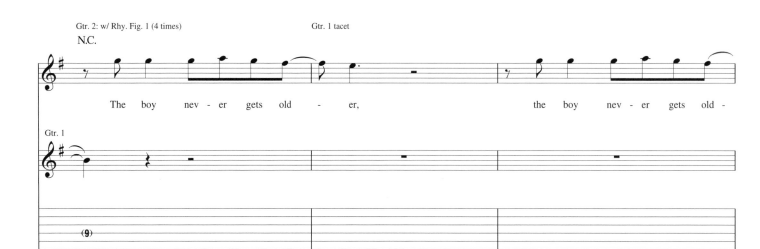

Gtr. 2: w/ Rhy. Fig. 1 (4 times)   Gtr. 1 tacet

N.C.

The boy nev - er gets old - er,   the boy nev - er gets old -

Gtr. 1

(9)

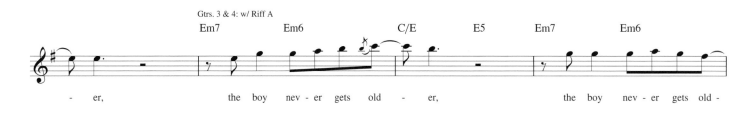

Gtrs. 3 & 4: w/ Riff A

Em7   Em6   C/E   E5   Em7   Em6

- er,   the boy nev - er gets old - er,   the boy nev - er gets old -

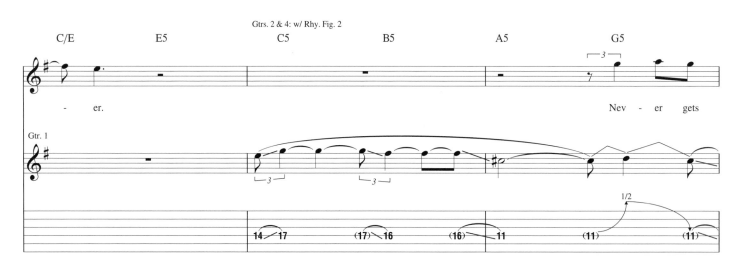

Gtrs. 2 & 4: w/ Rhy. Fig. 2

C/E   E5   C5   B5   A5   G5

- er.   Nev - er gets

Gtr. 1

14 17   (17) 16   (16) 11   (11)   (11)

1/2

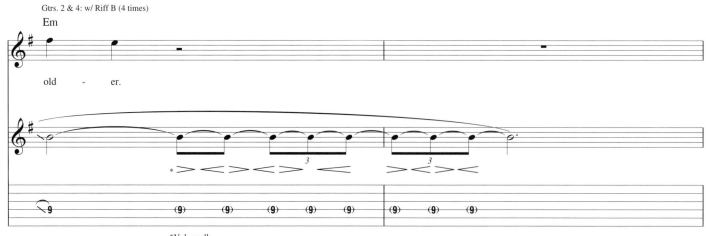

Gtrs. 2 & 4: w/ Riff B (4 times)

Em

old - er.

Gtr. 1

* > < > < > <   > < > <

(9)   (9) (9) (9) (9) (9)   (9) (9) (9)

*Vol. swells

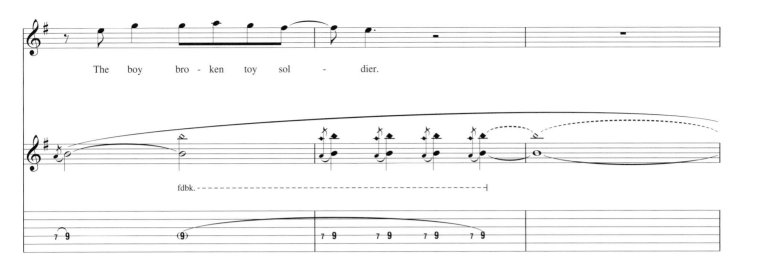

The boy bro-ken toy sol - dier.

fdbk.

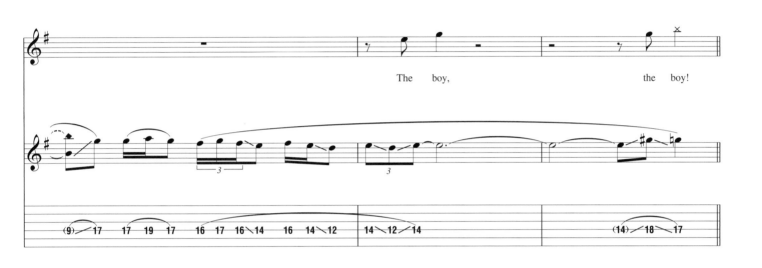

The boy,   the boy!

Outro
Gtrs. 2 & 4: w/ Rhy. Fig. 2

| E5 | C5 | B5 | A5 | G5 |

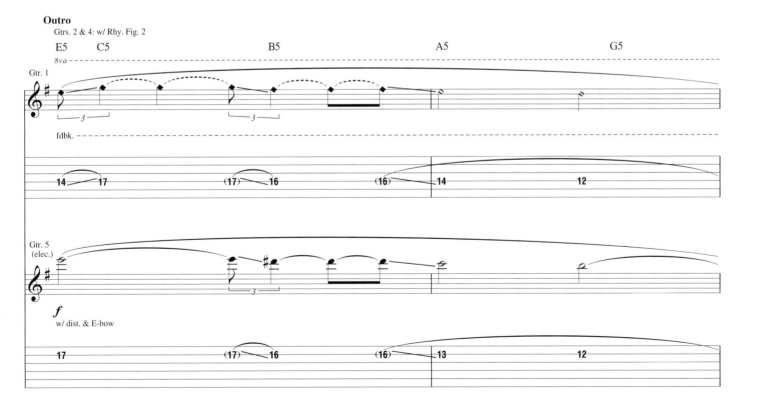

8va

Gtr. 1

fdbk.

Gtr. 5
(elec.)

f
w/ dist. & E-bow

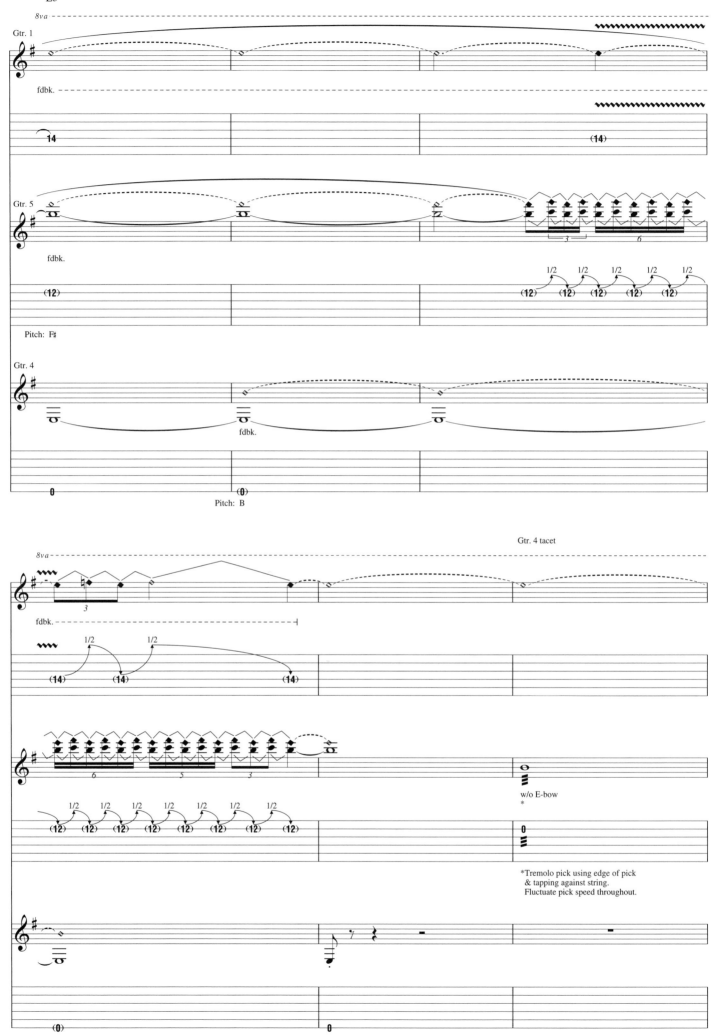

*Tremolo pick using edge of pick
& tapping against string.
Fluctuate pick speed throughout.

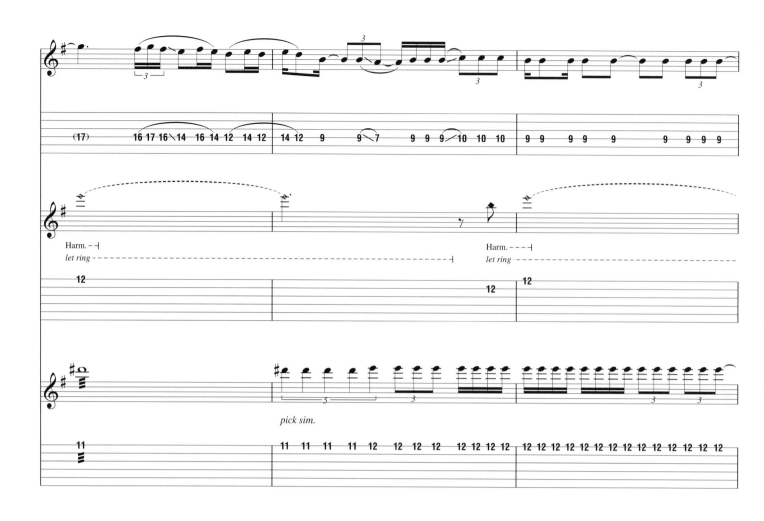

Free time

Gtrs. 3 & 5 tacet

Fade out

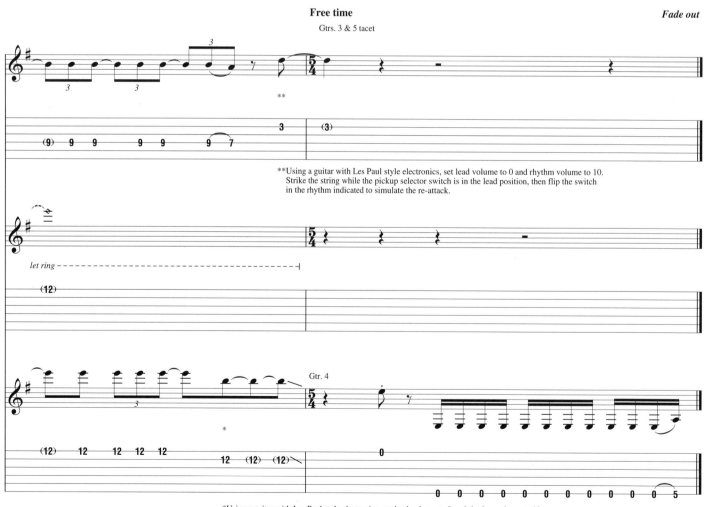

**Using a guitar with Les Paul style electronics, set lead volume to 0 and rhythm volume to 10.
Strike the string while the pickup selector switch is in the lead position, then flip the switch
in the rhythm indicated to simulate the re-attack.

Gtr. 4

*Using a guitar with Les Paul style electronics, set lead volume to 0 and rhythm volume to 10.
Strike the string while the pickup selector switch is in the lead position, then flip the switch
in the rhythm indicated to simulate the re-attack.

Intimate Secretary

Words and Music by Brendan Benson and Jack White

Gtr. 1: Open G tuning, up 1/4 step:
(low to high) D-G-D-G-B-D

Gtrs. 2 & 3: Tune up 1/4 step

Intro
Free time

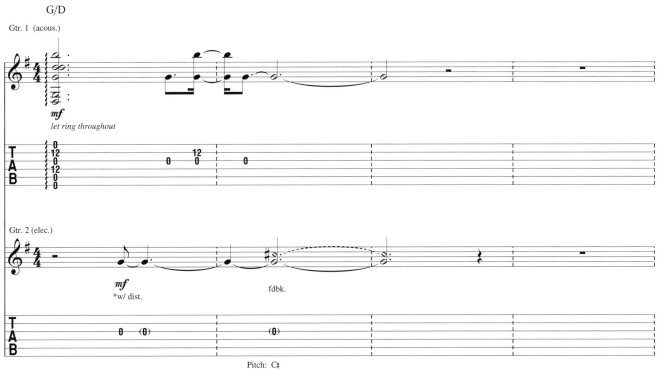

*Using a guitar with Les Paul style electronics, set lead volume to 0 and rhythm volume to 10.
Strike the string while the pickup selector switch is in the lead position, then flip the switch
in the rhythm indicated to simulate the re-attack.

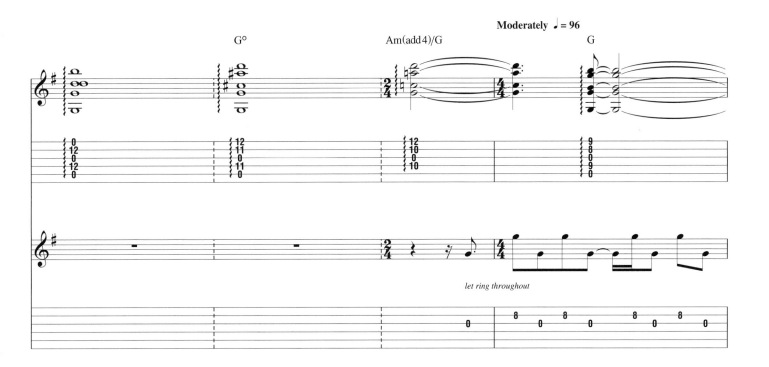

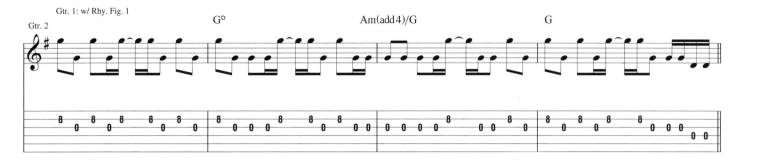

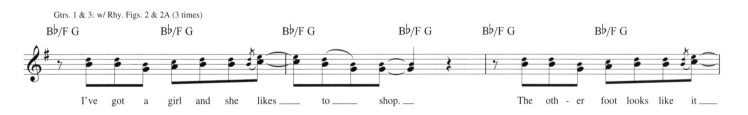

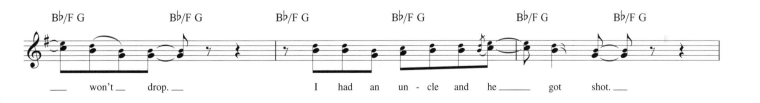

Together

Words and Music by Brendan Benson and Jack White

Tune up 1/4 step

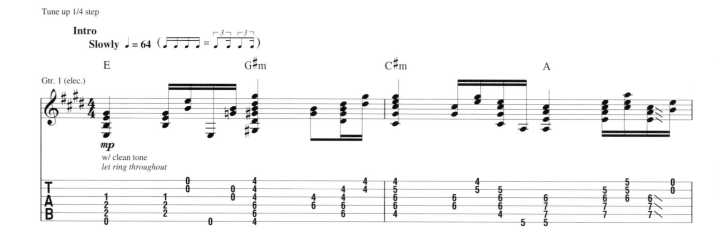

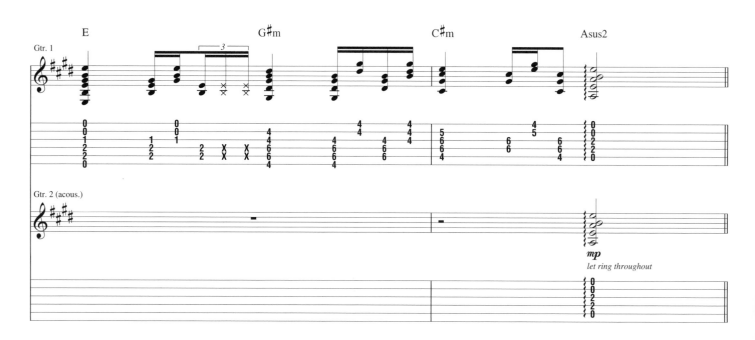

*Composite arrangement

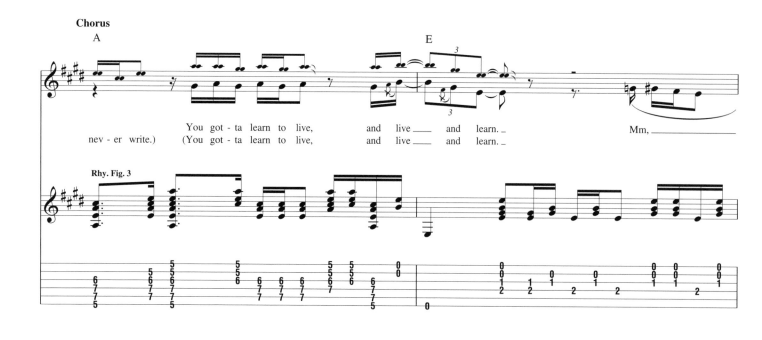

You got-ta learn to live, and live ___ and learn. ___
nev-er write.) (You got-ta learn to live, and live ___ and learn. ___
Mm, ___

Rhy. Fig. 3

you got-ta learn to give and wait ___ your turn ___ or you'll get
You got-ta learn to give and wait ___ your turn ___ or you'll get

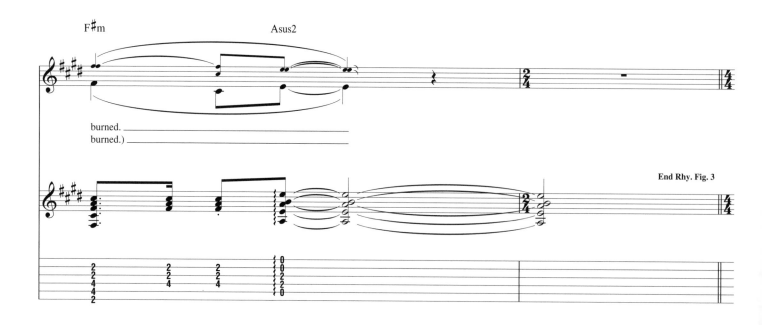

burned. _____
burned.) _____

End Rhy. Fig. 3

*Played as even sixteenth notes.

**As before

Level

Words and Music by Brendan Benson and Jack White

*Key signature denotes G Mixolydian.
**w/ ring modulator, next 4 1/2 meas.
***Synth. arr. for gtr.
†Chord symbols reflect implied harmony.

††Elec. piano arr. for gtr.
†††Brendan Benson - full size notes, Jack White - cue size notes.

nar - row.   I'm guess-in' all the time. ___   But I can't see the road ___   (if) I'm look-in' at the

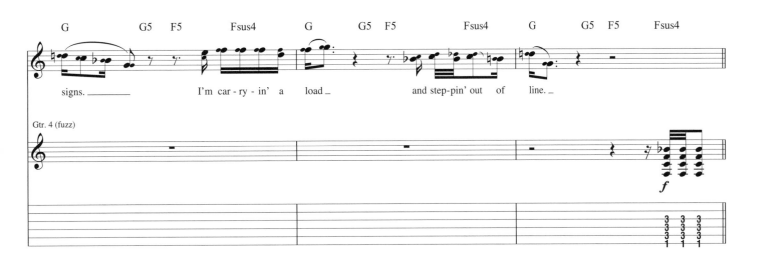

signs. ___   I'm car - ry - in' a load ___   and step-pin' out of line.

Gtr. 4 (fuzz)

Interlude

Gtr. 1: w/ Riff A (2 times)

Guitar Solo

Store Bought Bones

Words and Music by Brendan Benson and Jack White

Tune down 1/4 step

*Organ arr. for gtr.

**Vol. swell

***Vol. swell

†Chord symbols reflect implied harmony.

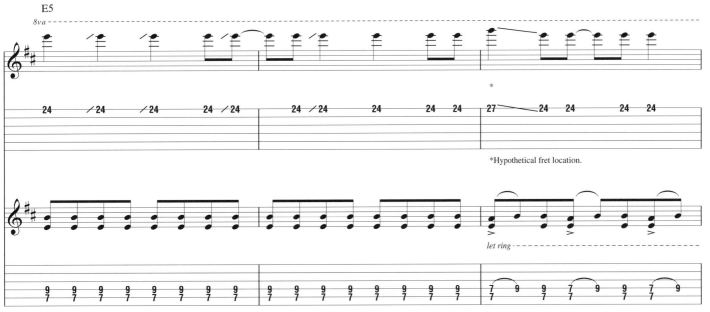

*Hypothetical fret location.

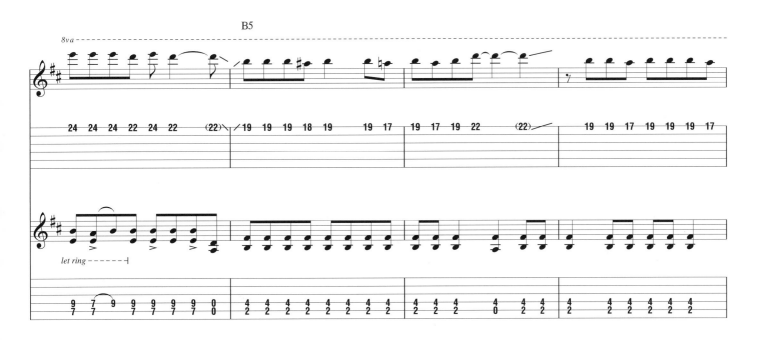

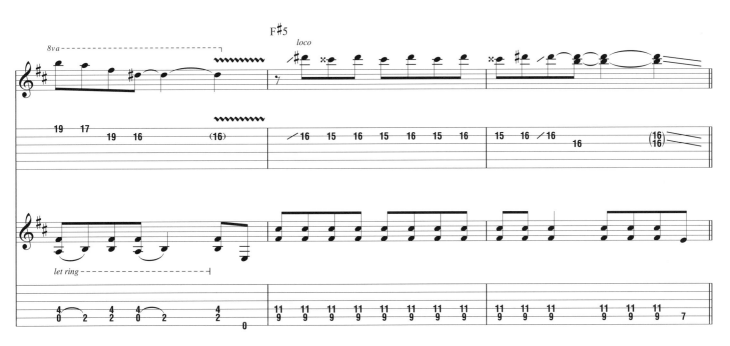

Outro

*Chord symbols implied by bass, next 2 meas.

Yellow Sun

Words and Music by Brendan Benson and Jack White

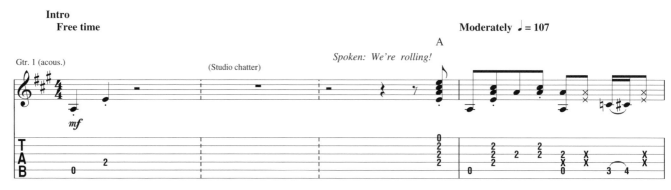

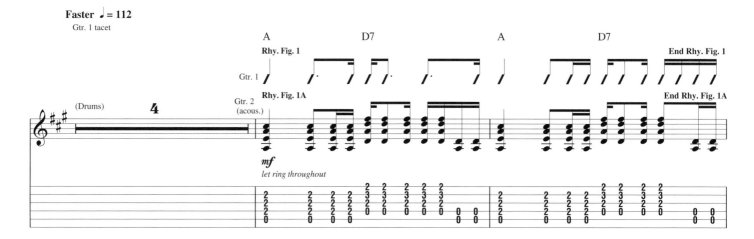

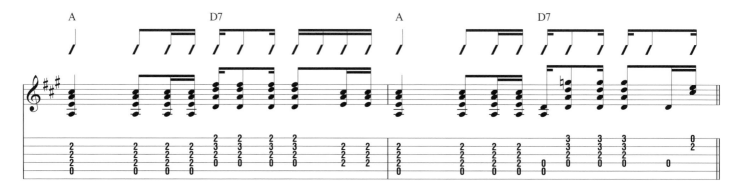

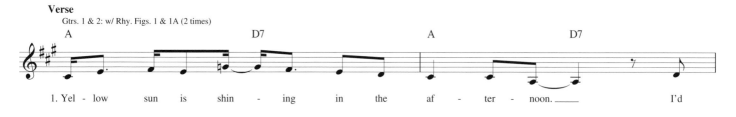

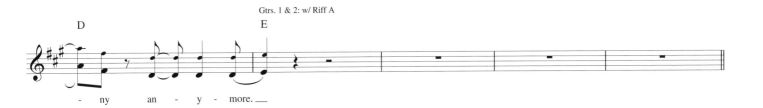

- ny   an - y - more. ___

Outro

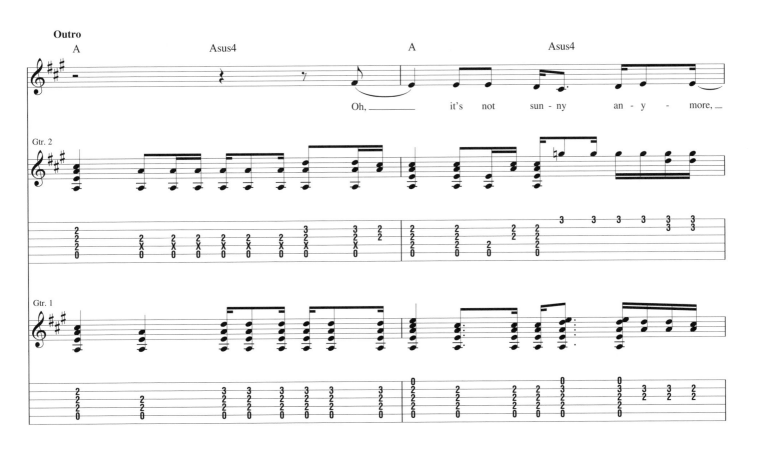

Oh, ___ it's not sun - ny an - y - more, ___

___ it's not sun - ny an - y - more, ___ it's not sun - ny an - y - more, ___

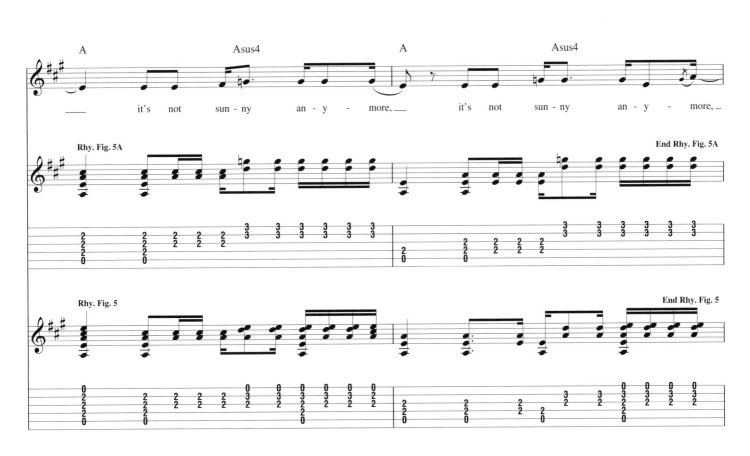

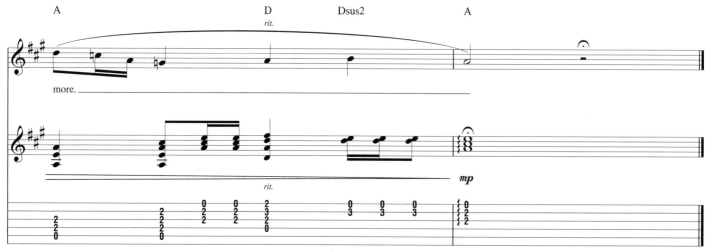

Call It a Day

Words and Music by Brendan Benson and Jack White

Coda 1

Gtr. 1: w/ Rhy. Fig. 2 (last 2 meas.)

F5   G

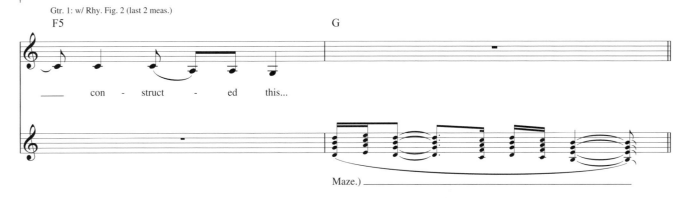

___ con - struct - ed this...

Maze.) _____

Verse

Gtr. 1: w/ Rhy. Fig. 1 (2 times)

C5   G5   C5   G5

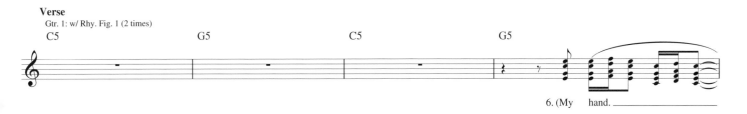

6. (My hand. _____

D.S.S. al Coda 2
(take 1st ending)

Gtr. 1: w/ Rhy. Fig. 2

C5   G5   F5   G

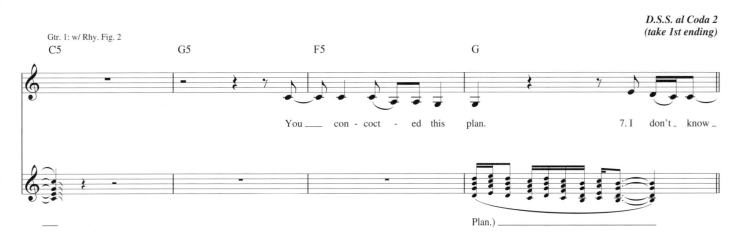

You ___ con - coct - ed this plan. 7. I don't_ know _

___   Plan.) _____

Coda 2

F5   G   F5   G

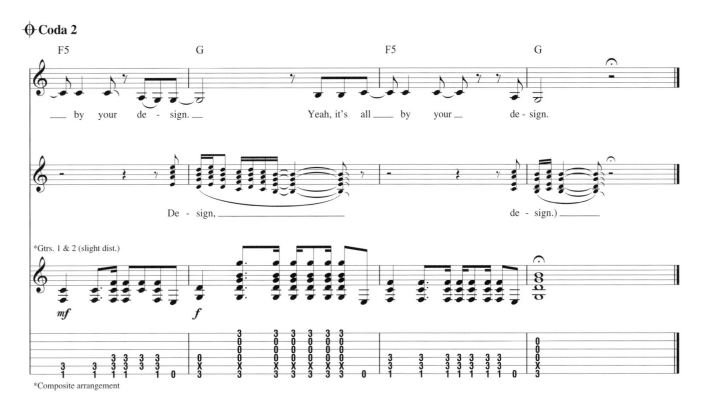

___ by your de - sign. _ Yeah, it's all _ by your _ de - sign.

De - sign, _____   de - sign.) _____

*Gtrs. 1 & 2 (slight dist.)

mf   *f*

*Composite arrangement

Blue Veins

Words and Music by Brendan Benson and Jack White

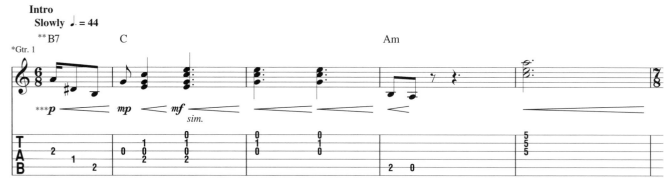

*Bkwds. gtr. arr. for regular gtr.
**Chord symbols reflect overall harmony.
***Vol. swells

Gtr. 1 tacet

Your blue vein.

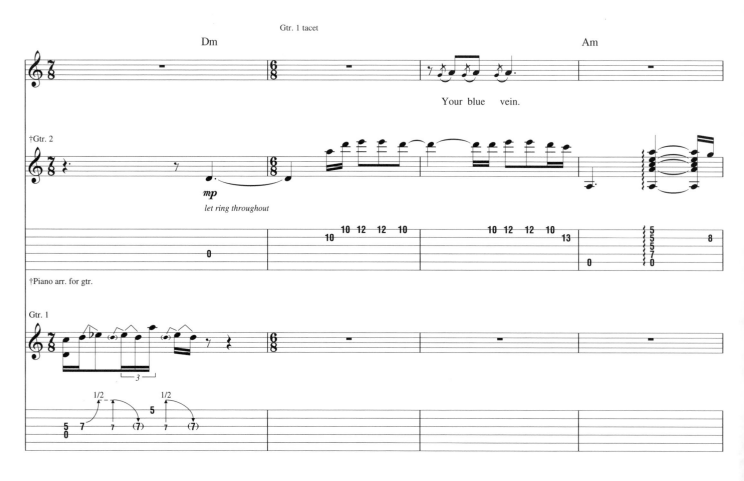

†Piano arr. for gtr.

B7

just in time   to see you smil-in' back at me and say-in', "Ev-'ry-thing's o - kay   as long as you're in-side my blue veins." _

let ring

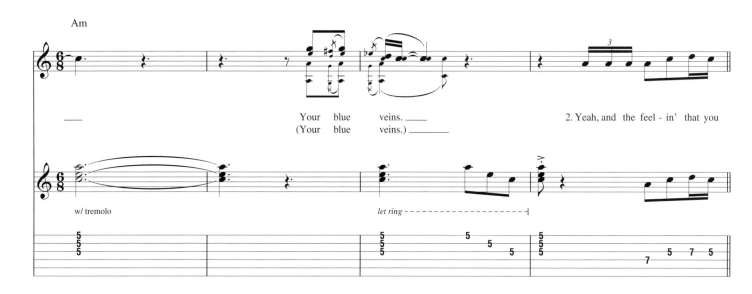

Am

    Your   blue   veins. _
(Your   blue   veins.) _

2. Yeah, and the feel - in' that you

w/ tremolo   *let ring*

% Verse

1st time, Gtr. 3: w/ Rhy. Fig. 2
2nd time, Gtr. 3: w/ Rhy. Fill 1
2nd time, Bkgd. Voc. tacet

2nd time, Gtr. 3: w/ Rhy. Fig. 2 (last 4 meas.)

Dm   Am

gave me,   (no) mat - ter   what I do or where I go,   it   al - ways will re - main. _
ceive me   like the   rest   and there's noth-in' you need to ex - plain. _

Voc. Fig. 1

(Oo, _   oo, _   oo.) _

Rhy. Fill 1
Gtr. 3

let ring

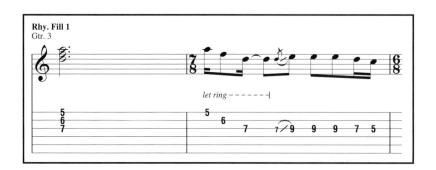

Your blue veins. _____
(Your blue veins.) _____

let ring - - - - - - - -

Bridge

w/ bkwds. vocs., next 5 meas.
Gtr. 3 tacet

Gtr. 1 tacet

Am   Dm   Am

Gtr. 1

Gtr. 2

Gtr. 3: w/ Rhy. Fig. 1

Mm, _____ think it's gon-na rain. _

Gtr. 2

pp

Gtr. 2 tacet

Your blue veins. _____
(Your blue veins.) _____

3. And I know you won't de -

⊕ Coda

Am

ain't noth-in' com-pared ___ to the love _____ that's run-nin' through your lit-tle blue veins, eh.

let ring -

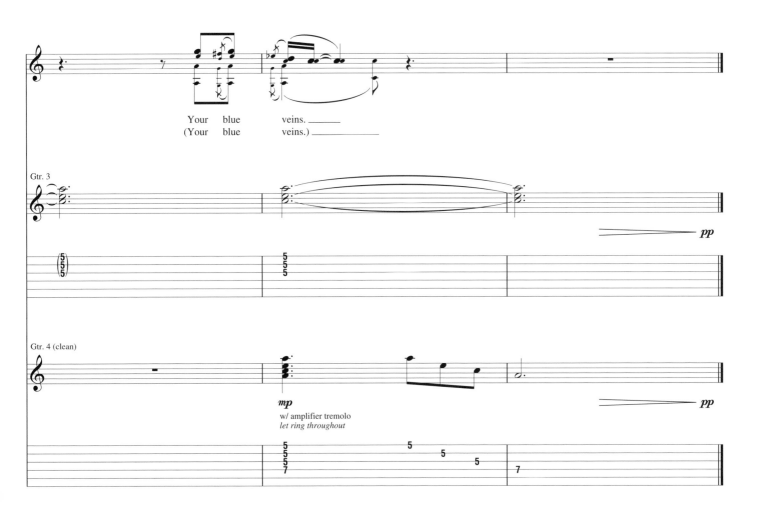

Your blue veins. _____
(Your blue veins.) _____

Gtr. 3

pp

Gtr. 4 (clean)

mp

w/ amplifier tremolo
let ring throughout

pp

Guitar Notation Legend

Guitar music can be notated three different ways: on a *musical staff*, in *tablature*, and in *rhythm slashes*.

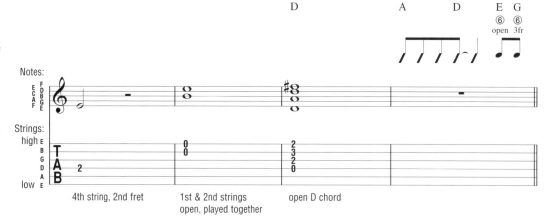

RHYTHM SLASHES are written above the staff. Strum chords in the rhythm indicated. Use the chord diagrams found at the top of the first page of the transcription for the appropriate chord voicings. Round noteheads indicate single notes.

THE MUSICAL STAFF shows pitches and rhythms and is divided by bar lines into measures. Pitches are named after the first seven letters of the alphabet.

TABLATURE graphically represents the guitar fingerboard. Each horizontal line represents a string, and each number represents a fret.

4th string, 2nd fret

1st & 2nd strings open, played together

open D chord

Definitions for Special Guitar Notation

HALF-STEP BEND: Strike the note and bend up 1/2 step.

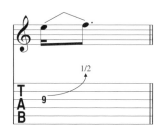

WHOLE-STEP BEND: Strike the note and bend up one step.

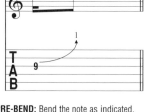

GRACE NOTE BEND: Strike the note and immediately bend up as indicated.

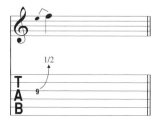

SLIGHT (MICROTONE) BEND: Strike the note and bend up 1/4 step.

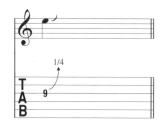

BEND AND RELEASE: Strike the note and bend up as indicated, then release back to the original note. Only the first note is struck.

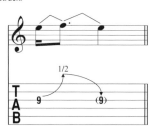

PRE-BEND: Bend the note as indicated, then strike it.

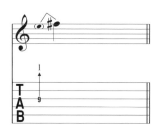

PRE-BEND AND RELEASE: Bend the note as indicated. Strike it and release the bend back to the original note.

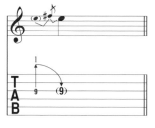

UNISON BEND: Strike the two notes simultaneously and bend the lower note up to the pitch of the higher.

VIBRATO: The string is vibrated by rapidly bending and releasing the note with the fretting hand.

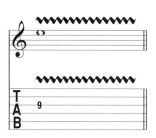

WIDE VIBRATO: The pitch is varied to a greater degree by vibrating with the fretting hand.

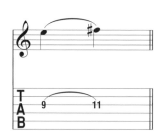

HAMMER-ON: Strike the first (lower) note with one finger, then sound the higher note (on the same string) with another finger by fretting it without picking.

PULL-OFF: Place both fingers on the notes to be sounded. Strike the first note and without picking, pull the finger off to sound the second (lower) note.

LEGATO SLIDE: Strike the first note and then slide the same fret-hand finger up or down to the second note. The second note is not struck.

SHIFT SLIDE: Same as legato slide, except the second note is struck.

TRILL: Very rapidly alternate between the notes indicated by continuously hammering on and pulling off.

TAPPING: Hammer ("tap") the fret indicated with the pick-hand index or middle finger and pull off to the note fretted by the fret hand.

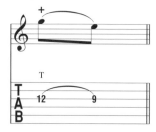

74

NATURAL HARMONIC: Strike the note while the fret-hand lightly touches the string directly over the fret indicated.

PINCH HARMONIC: The note is fretted normally and a harmonic is produced by adding the edge of the thumb or the tip of the index finger of the pick hand to the normal pick attack.

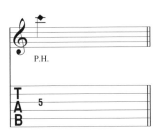

HARP HARMONIC: The note is fretted normally and a harmonic is produced by gently resting the pick hand's index finger directly above the indicated fret (in parentheses) while the pick hand's thumb or pick assists by plucking the appropriate string.

PICK SCRAPE: The edge of the pick is rubbed down (or up) the string, producing a scratchy sound.

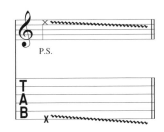

MUFFLED STRINGS: A percussive sound is produced by laying the fret hand across the string(s) without depressing, and striking them with the pick hand.

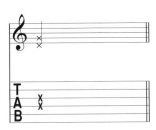

PALM MUTING: The note is partially muted by the pick hand lightly touching the string(s) just before the bridge.

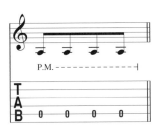

RAKE: Drag the pick across the strings indicated with a single motion.

TREMOLO PICKING: The note is picked as rapidly and continuously as possible.

ARPEGGIATE: Play the notes of the chord indicated by quickly rolling them from bottom to top.

VIBRATO BAR DIVE AND RETURN: The pitch of the note or chord is dropped a specified number of steps (in rhythm), then returned to the original pitch.

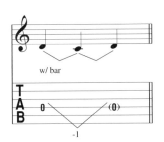

VIBRATO BAR SCOOP: Depress the bar just before striking the note, then quickly release the bar.

VIBRATO BAR DIP: Strike the note and then immediately drop a specified number of steps, then release back to the original pitch.

Additional Musical Definitions

 *(accent)* • Accentuate note (play it louder).

 *(accent)* • Accentuate note with great intensity.

 *(staccato)* • Play the note short.

 • Downstroke

∨ • Upstroke

D.S. al Coda • Go back to the sign (𝄋), then play until the measure marked "*To Coda*," then skip to the section labelled "**Coda**."

D.C. al Fine • Go back to the beginning of the song and play until the measure marked "*Fine*" (end).

Rhy. Fig. • Label used to recall a recurring accompaniment pattern (usually chordal).

Riff • Label used to recall composed, melodic lines (usually single notes) which recur.

Fill • Label used to identify a brief melodic figure which is to be inserted into the arrangement.

Rhy. Fill • A chordal version of a Fill.

tacet • Instrument is silent (drops out).

• Repeat measures between signs.

• When a repeated section has different endings, play the first ending only the first time and the second ending only the second time.

NOTE: Tablature numbers in parentheses mean:
1. The note is being sustained over a system (note in standard notation is tied), or
2. The note is sustained, but a new articulation (such as a hammer-on, pull-off, slide or vibrato) begins, or
3. The note is a barely audible "ghost" note (note in standard notation is also in parentheses).

GUITAR RECORDED VERSIONS®

Guitar Recorded Versions® are note-for-note transcriptions of guitar music taken directly off recordings. This series, one of the most popular in print today, features some of the greatest guitar players and groups from blues and rock to country and jazz.

Guitar Recorded Versions are transcribed by the best transcribers in the business. Every book contains notes and tablature.

AUTHENTIC TRANSCRIPTIONS WITH NOTES AND TABLATURE

RECORDED VERSIONS GUITAR

AUTHENTIC TRANSCRIPTIONS WITH NOTES AND TABLATURE

00694757 Yngwie Malmsteen – Trilogy $19.95
00690754 Marilyn Manson – Lest We Forget $19.95
00694956 Bob Marley – Legend $19.95
00690075 Bob Marley – Natural Mystic $19.95
00690548 Very Best of Bob Marley & The Wailers – One Love $19.95
00694945 Bob Marley – Songs of Freedom $24.95
00690748 Maroon5 – 1.22.03 Acoustic $19.95
00690657 Maroon5 – Songs About Jane $19.95
00690442 Matchbox 20 – Mad Season $19.95
00690616 Matchbox 20 – More Than You Think You Are ..$19.95
00690239 Matchbox 20 – Yourself or Someone Like You ..$19.95
00690283 Best of Sarah McLachlan $19.95
00690382 Sarah McLachlan – Mirrorball $19.95
00690354 Sarah McLachlan – Surfacing $19.95
00120080 Don McLean Songbook $19.95
00694952 Megadeth – Countdown to Extinction $19.95
00690244 Megadeth – Cryptic Writings $19.95
00694951 Megadeth – Rust in Peace $22.95
00694953 Megadeth – Selections from Peace Sells...But Who's Buying? & So Far, So Good...So What! $22.95
00690768 Megadeth – The System Has Failed $19.95
00690495 Megadeth – The World Needs a Hero $19.95
00690011 Megadeth – Youthanasia $19.95
00690505 John Mellencamp Guitar Collection $19.95
00690562 Pat Metheny – Bright Size Life $19.95
00690646 Pat Metheny – One Quiet Night $19.95
00690559 Pat Metheny – Question & Answer $19.95
00690565 Pat Metheny – Rejoicing $19.95
00690558 Pat Metheny Trio – 99>00 ....$19.95
00690561 Pat Metheny Trio – Live $22.95
00690040 Steve Miller Band Greatest Hits $19.95
00690769 Modest Mouse – Good News for People Who Love Bad News $19.95
00694802 Gary Moore – Still Got the Blues $19.95
00690103 Alanis Morissette – Jagged Little Pill $19.95
00690786 Mudvayne – The End of All Things to Come $22.95
00690787 Mudvayne – L.D. 50 ....$22.95
00690794 Mudvayne – Lost and Found $19.95
00690448 MxPx – The Ever Passing Moment $19.95
00690500 Ricky Nelson Guitar Collection $17.95
00690722 New Found Glory – Catalyst $19.95
00690345 Best of Newsboys $17.95
00690611 Nirvana $22.95
00694895 Nirvana – Bleach $19.95
00690189 Nirvana – From the Muddy Banks of the Wishkah $19.95
00694913 Nirvana – In Utero $19.95
00694901 Nirvana – Incesticide $19.95
00694883 Nirvana – Nevermind $19.95
00690026 Nirvana – Unplugged in York $19.95
00690739 No Doubt – Rock Steady $22.95
00120112 No Doubt – Tragic Kingdom $22.95
00690273 Oasis – Be Here Now $19.95
00690159 Oasis – Definitely Maybe $19.95
00690121 Oasis – (What's the Story) Morning Glory $19.95
00690226 Oasis – The Other Side of Oasis $19.95
00690358 The Offspring – Americana $19.95
00690485 The Offspring – Conspiracy of One $19.95
00690807 The Offspring – Greatest Hits $19.95
00690204 The Offspring – Ixnay on the Hombre $17.95
00690203 The Offspring – Smash $18.95
00690663 The Offspring – Splinter $19.95
00694847 Best of Ozzy Osbourne $22.95
00694830 Ozzy Osbourne – No More Tears $19.95
00690399 Ozzy Osbourne – The Ozzman Cometh $19.95
00690129 Ozzy Osbourne – Ozzmosis $22.95
00690594 Best of Les Paul $19.95
00690546 P.O.D. – Satellite $19.95
00694855 Pearl Jam – Ten $19.95
00690439 A Perfect Circle – Mer De Noms $19.95
00690661 A Perfect Circle – Thirteenth Step $19.95
00690499 Tom Petty – Definitive Guitar Collection $19.95
00690176 Phish – Billy Breathes $22.95
00690424 Phish – Farmhouse $19.95
00690240 Phish – Hoist $19.95
00690331 Phish – Story of the Ghost $19.95
00690642 Pillar – Fireproof $19.95
00690731 Pillar – Where Do We Go from Here $19.95
00690428 Pink Floyd – Dark Side of the Moon $19.95
00693864 Best of The Police $19.95
00690299 Best of Elvis: The King of Rock 'n' Roll $19.95
00692535 Elvis Presley $18.95
00690003 Classic Queen $24.95
00694975 Queen – Greatest Hits $24.95
00690670 Very Best of Queensryche $19.95
00694910 Rage Against the Machine $19.95
00690145 Rage Against the Machine – Evil Empire $19.95
00690179 Rancid – And Out Come the Wolves $22.95
00690426 Best of Ratt $19.95
00690055 Red Hot Chili Peppers – Bloodsugarsexmagik ..$19.95
00690584 Red Hot Chili Peppers – By the Way $19.95
00690379 Red Hot Chili Peppers – Californication $19.95
00690673 Red Hot Chili Peppers – Greatest Hits $19.95
00690255 Red Hot Chili Peppers – Mother's Milk $19.95
00690090 Red Hot Chili Peppers – One Hot Minute $22.95
00690511 Django Reinhardt – The Definitive Collection $19.95
00690779 Relient K – MMHMM $19.95
00690643 Relient K – Two Lefts Don't Make a Right ... But Three Do $19.95
00694899 R.E.M. – Automatic for the People $19.95
00690260 Jimmie Rodgers Guitar Collection $19.95
00690014 Rolling Stones – Exile on Main Street $24.95
00690631 Rolling Stones – Guitar Anthology $24.95
00690186 Rolling Stones – Rock & Roll Circus $19.95
00690685 David Lee Roth – Eat 'Em and Smile $19.95
00690694 David Lee Roth – Guitar Anthology $24.95
00690749 Saliva – Survival of the Sickest $19.95
00690031 Santana's Greatest Hits $19.95
00690796 Very Best of Michael Schenker $19.95
00690566 Best of Scorpions $19.95
00690604 Bob Seger – Guitar Anthology $19.95
00690659 Bob Seger and the Silver Bullet Band – Greatest Hits, Volume 2 ....$17.95
00120105 Kenny Wayne Shepherd – Ledbetter Heights $19.95
00690750 Kenny Wayne Shepherd – The Place You're In ..$19.95
00120123 Kenny Wayne Shepherd – Trouble Is $19.95
00690196 Silverchair – Freak Show $19.95
00690130 Silverchair – Frogstomp $19.95
00690357 Silverchair – Neon Ballroom $19.95
00690419 Slipknot $19.95
00690530 Slipknot – Iowa $19.95
00690733 Slipknot – Volume 3 (The Subliminal Verses) ..$19.95
00690691 Smashing Pumpkins Anthology $19.95
00690330 Social Distortion – Live at the Roxy $19.95
00120004 Best of Steely Dan $24.95
00694921 Best of Steppenwolf $22.95
00690655 Best of Mike Stern $19.95
00694801 Best of Rod Stewart $22.95
00694957 Rod Stewart – Unplugged...And Seated $22.95
00690021 Sting – Fields of Gold $19.95
00694955 Sting for Guitar Tab $19.95
00690597 Stone Sour $19.95
00690689 Story of the Year – Page Avenue $19.95
00690520 Styx Guitar Collection $19.95
00120081 Sublime $19.95
00690519 SUM 41 – All Killer No Filler $19.95
00690771 SUM 41 – Chuck $19.95
00690612 SUM 41 – Does This Look Infected? $19.95
00690767 Switchfoot – The Beautiful Letdown $19.95
00690815 Switchfoot – Nothing Is Sound $19.95
00690425 System of a Down $19.95
00690799 System of a Down – Mezmerize $19.95
00690606 System of a Down – Steal This Album $19.95
00690531 System of a Down – Toxicity $19.95
00694824 Best of James Taylor $16.95
00694887 Best of Thin Lizzy $19.95
00690238 Third Eye Blind $19.95
00690671 Three Days Grace $19.95
00690738 3 Doors Down – Away from the Sun $22.95
00690737 3 Doors Down – The Better Life $22.95
00690776 3 Doors Down – Seventeen Days $19.95
00690267 311 ....$19.95
00690580 311 – From Chaos $19.95
00690269 311 – Grass Roots $19.95
00690268 311 – Music $19.95
00690665 Thursday – War All the Time $19.95
00690030 Toad the Wet Sprocket $19.95
00690654 Best of Train $19.95
00690233 Merle Travis Collection $19.95
00690683 Robin Trower – Bridge of Sighs $19.95
00690740 Shania Twain – Guitar Collection $19.95
00699191 U2 – Best of: 1980-1990 ....$19.95
00690732 U2 – Best of: 1990-2000 ....$19.95
00690775 U2 – How to Dismantle an Atomic Bomb $22.95
00694411 U2 – The Joshua Tree $19.95
00690039 Steve Vai – Alien Love Secrets $24.95
00690172 Steve Vai – Fire Garden $24.95
00690343 Steve Vai – Flex-able Leftovers $19.95
00660137 Steve Vai – Passion & Warfare $24.95
00690605 Steve Vai – Selections from the Elusive Light and Sound, Volume 1 ....$24.95
00694904 Steve Vai – Sex and Religion $24.95
00690392 Steve Vai – The Ultra Zone $22.95
00690023 Jimmie Vaughan – Strange Pleasures $19.95
00690455 Stevie Ray Vaughan – Blues at Sunrise $19.95
00690024 Stevie Ray Vaughan – Couldn't Stand the Weather ..$19.95
00690370 Stevie Ray Vaughan and Double Trouble – The Real Deal: Greatest Hits Volume 2 ....$22.95
00690116 Stevie Ray Vaughan – Guitar Collection $24.95
00660136 Stevie Ray Vaughan – In Step $19.95
00694879 Stevie Ray Vaughan – In the Beginning $19.95
00660058 Stevie Ray Vaughan – Lightnin' Blues '83-'87 ....$24.95
00690036 Stevie Ray Vaughan – Live Alive $24.95
00690417 Stevie Ray Vaughan – Live at Carnegie Hall $19.95
00690550 Stevie Ray Vaughan and Double Trouble – Live at Montreux 1982 & 1985 ....$24.95
00694835 Stevie Ray Vaughan – The Sky Is Crying $22.95
00690025 Stevie Ray Vaughan – Soul to Soul $19.95
00690015 Stevie Ray Vaughan – Texas Flood $19.95
00694776 Vaughan Brothers – Family Style $19.95
00690772 Velvet Revolver – Contraband $19.95
00690132 The T-Bone Walker Collection $19.95
00694789 Muddy Waters – Deep Blues $24.95
00690071 Weezer (The Blue Album) $19.95
00690516 Weezer (The Green Album) $19.95
00690800 Weezer – Make Believe $19.95
00690286 Weezer – Pinkerton $19.95
00690447 Best of The Who $24.95
00694970 The Who – Definitive Guitar Collection: A-E $24.95
00694971 The Who – Definitive Guitar Collection: F-Li $24.95
00694972 The Who – Definitive Guitar Collection: Lo-R $24.95
00694973 The Who – Definitive Guitar Collection: S-Y $24.95
00690640 David Wilcox – Anthology 2000-2003 ....$19.95
00690325 David Wilcox – Collection $17.95
00690672 Best of Dar Williams $19.95
00690320 Dar Williams Songbook $17.95
00690319 Stevie Wonder – Some of the Best $17.95
00690596 Best of the Yardbirds $19.95
00690710 Yellowcard – Ocean Avenue $19.95
00690507 Frank Zappa – Apostrophe $19.95
00690443 Frank Zappa – Hot Rats $19.95
00690589 ZZ Top – Guitar Anthology $22.95

FOR MORE INFORMATION, SEE YOUR LOCAL MUSIC DEALER, OR WRITE TO:

HAL•LEONARD® CORPORATION

7777 W. BLUEMOUND RD. P.O. BOX 13819 MILWAUKEE, WI 53213

Complete songlists and more at **www.halleonard.com**

Prices, contents, and availability subject to change without notice.

0106

HAL•LEONARD GUITAR PLAY•ALONG

This series will help you play your favorite songs quickly and easily. Just follow the tab and listen to the CD to hear how the guitar should sound, and then play along using the separate backing tracks. Mac or PC users can also slow down the tempo without changing pitch by using the CD in their computer. The melody and lyrics are included in the book so that you can sing or simply follow along.

INCLUDES TAB

VOL. 1 – ROCK GUITAR   00699570 / $14.95
Day Tripper • Message in a Bottle • Refugee • Shattered • Sunshine of Your Love • Takin' Care of Business • Tush • Walk This Way.

VOL. 2 – ACOUSTIC   00699569 / $14.95
Angie • Behind Blue Eyes • Best of My Love • Blackbird • Dust in the Wind • Layla • Night Moves • Yesterday.

VOL. 3 – HARD ROCK   00699573 / $14.95
Crazy Train • Iron Man • Living After Midnight • Rock You like a Hurricane • Round and Round • Smoke on the Water • Sweet Child O' Mine • You Really Got Me.

VOL. 4 – POP/ROCK   00699571 / $14.95
Breakdown • Crazy Little Thing Called Love • Hit Me with Your Best Shot • I Want You to Want Me • Lights • R.O.C.K. in the U.S.A. • Summer of '69 • What I Like About You.

VOL. 5 – MODERN ROCK   00699574 / $14.95
Aerials • Alive • Bother • Chop Suey! • Control • Last Resort • Take a Look Around (Theme from *M:I-2*) • Wish You Were Here.

VOL. 6 – '90S ROCK   00699572 / $14.95
Are You Gonna Go My Way • Come Out and Play • I'll Stick Around • Know Your Enemy • Man in the Box • Outshined • Smells Like Teen Spirit • Under the Bridge.

VOL. 7 – BLUES GUITAR   00699575 / $14.95
All Your Love (I Miss Loving) • Born Under a Bad Sign • Hide Away • I'm Tore Down • I'm Your Hoochie Coochie Man • Pride and Joy • Sweet Home Chicago • The Thrill Is Gone.

VOL. 8 – ROCK   00699585 / $14.95
All Right Now • Black Magic Woman • Get Back • Hey Joe • Layla • Love Me Two Times • Won't Get Fooled Again • You Really Got Me.

VOL. 9 – PUNK ROCK   00699576 / $14.95
All the Small Things • Fat Lip • Flavor of the Weak • I Feel So • Lifestyles of the Rich and Famous• Say It Ain't So • Self Esteem • (So) Tired of Waiting for You.

VOL. 10 – ACOUSTIC   00699586 / $14.95
Here Comes the Sun • Landslide • The Magic Bus • Norwegian Wood (This Bird Has Flown) • Pink Houses • Space Oddity • Tangled Up in Blue • Tears in Heaven.

VOL. 11 – EARLY ROCK   00699579 / $14.95
Fun, Fun, Fun • Hound Dog • Louie, Louie • No Particular Place to Go • Oh, Pretty Woman • Rock Around the Clock • Under the Boardwalk • Wild Thing.

VOL. 12 – POP/ROCK   00699587 / $14.95
867-5309/Jenny • Every Breath You Take • Money for Nothing • Rebel, Rebel • Run to You • Ticket to Ride • Wonderful Tonight • You Give Love a Bad Name.

VOL. 13 – FOLK ROCK   00699581 / $14.95
Annie's Song • Leaving on a Jet Plane • Suite: Judy Blue Eyes • This Land Is Your Land • Time in a Bottle • Turn! Turn! Turn! • You've Got a Friend • You've Got to Hide Your Love Away.

VOL. 14 – BLUES ROCK   00699582 / $14.95
Blue on Black • Crossfire • Cross Road Blues (Crossroads) • The House Is Rockin' • La Grange • Move It on Over • Roadhouse Blues • Statesboro Blues.

VOL. 15 – R&B   00699583 / $14.95
Ain't Too Proud to Beg • Brick House • Get Ready • I Can't Help Myself • I Got You (I Feel Good) • I Heard It Through the Grapevine • My Girl • Shining Star.

VOL. 16 – JAZZ   00699584 / $14.95
All Blues • Bluesette • Footprints • How Insensitive • Misty • Satin Doll • Stella by Starlight • Tenor Madness.

VOL. 17 – COUNTRY   00699588 / $14.95
Amie • Boot Scootin' Boogie • Chattahoochee • Folsom Prison Blues • Friends in Low Places • Forever and Ever, Amen • T-R-O-U-B-L-E • Workin' Man Blues.

VOL. 18 – ACOUSTIC ROCK   00699577 / $14.95
About a Girl • Breaking the Girl • Drive • Iris • More Than Words • Patience • Silent Lucidity • 3 AM.

VOL. 19 – SOUL   00699578 / $14.95
Get Up (I Feel Like Being) a Sex Machine • Green Onions • In the Midnight Hour • Knock on Wood • Mustang Sally • Respect • (Sittin' On) The Dock of the Bay • Soul Man.

VOL. 20 – ROCKABILLY   00699580 / $14.95
Be-Bop-A-Lula • Blue Suede Shoes • Hello Mary Lou • Little Sister • Mystery Train • Rock This Town • Stray Cat Strut • That'll Be the Day.

VOL. 21 – YULETIDE   00699602 / $14.95
Angels We Have Heard on High • Away in a Manger • Deck the Hall • The First Noel • Go, Tell It on the Mountain • Jingle Bells • Joy to the World • O Little Town of Bethlehem.

VOL. 22 – CHRISTMAS   00699600 / $14.95
The Christmas Song • Frosty the Snow Man • Happy Xmas • Here Comes Santa Claus • Jingle-Bell Rock • Merry Christmas, Darling • Rudolph the Red-Nosed Reindeer • Silver Bells.

VOL. 23 – SURF   00699635 / $14.95
Let's Go Trippin' • Out of Limits • Penetration • Pipeline • Surf City • Surfin' U.S.A. • Walk Don't Run • The Wedge.

VOL. 24 – ERIC CLAPTON   00699649 / $14.95
Badge • Bell Bottom Blues • Change the World • Cocaine • Key to the Highway • Lay Down Sally • White Room • Wonderful Tonight.

VOL. 25 – LENNON & McCARTNEY   00699642 / $14.95
Back in the U.S.S.R. • Drive My Car • Get Back • A Hard Day's Night • I Feel Fine • Paperback Writer • Revolution • Ticket to Ride.

VOL. 26 – ELVIS PRESLEY   00699643 / $14.95
All Shook Up • Blue Suede Shoes • Don't Be Cruel • Heartbreak Hotel • Hound Dog • Jailhouse Rock • Little Sister • Mystery Train.

VOL. 27 – DAVID LEE ROTH   00699645 / $14.95
Ain't Talkin' 'Bout Love • Dance the Night Away • Hot for Teacher • Just Like Paradise • A Lil' Ain't Enough • Runnin' with the Devil • Unchained • Yankee Rose.

VOL. 28 – GREG KOCH   00699646 / $14.95
Chief's Blues • Death of a Bassman • Dylan the Villain • The Grip • Holy Grail • Spank It • Tonus Diabolicus • Zoiks.

VOL. 29 – BOB SEGER   00699647 / $14.95
Against the Wind • Betty Lou's Gettin' Out Tonight • Hollywood Nights • Mainstreet • Night Moves • Old Time Rock & Roll • Rock and Roll Never Forgets • Still the Same.

VOL. 30 – KISS   00699644 / $14.95
Cold Gin • Detroit Rock City • Deuce • Firehouse • Heaven's on Fire • Love Gun • Rock and Roll All Nite • Shock Me.

VOL. 31 – CHRISTMAS HITS   00699652 / $14.95
Blue Christmas • Do You Hear What I Hear • Happy Holiday • I Saw Mommy Kissing Santa Claus • I'll Be Home for Christmas • Let It Snow! Let It Snow! Let It Snow! • Little Saint Nick • Snowfall.

VOL. 32 – THE OFFSPRING   00699653 / $14.95
Bad Habit • Come Out and Play • Gone Away • Gotta Get Away • Hit That • The Kids Aren't Alright • Pretty Fly (For a White Guy) • Self Esteem.

VOL. 33 – ACOUSTIC CLASSICS   00699656 / $14.95
Across the Universe • Babe, I'm Gonna Leave You • Crazy on You • Heart of Gold • Hotel California • I'd Love to Change the World • Thick As a Brick • Wanted Dead or Alive.

VOL. 34 – CLASSIC ROCK   00699658 / $14.95
Aqualung • Born to Be Wild • The Boys Are Back in Town • Brown Eyed Girl • Reeling in the Years • Rock'n Me • Rocky Mountain Way • Sweet Emotion.

VOL. 35 – HAIR METAL   00699660 / $14.95
Decadence Dance • Don't Treat Me Bad • Down Boys • Seventeen • Shake Me • Up All Night • Wait • Talk Dirty to Me.

VOL. 36 – SOUTHERN ROCK   00699661 / $14.95
Can't You See • Flirtin' with Disaster • Hold on Loosely • Jessica • Mississippi Queen • Ramblin' Man • Sweet Home Alabama • What's Your Name.

VOL. 37 – ACOUSTIC METAL   00699662 / $14.95
Every Rose Has Its Thorn • Fly to the Angels • Hole Hearted • Love Is on the Way • Love of a Lifetime • Signs • To Be with You • When the Children Cry.

VOL. 38 – BLUES   00699663 / $14.95
Boom Boom • Cold Shot • Crosscut Saw • Everyday I Have the Blues • Frosty • Further On up the Road • Killing Floor • Texas Flood.

VOL. 39 – '80S METAL   00699664 / $14.95
Bark at the Moon • Big City Nights • Breaking the Chains • Cult of Personality • Lay It Down • Living on a Prayer • Panama • Smokin' in the Boys Room.

VOL. 40 – INCUBUS   00699668 / $14.95
Are You In? • Drive • Megalomaniac • Nice to Know You • Pardon Me • Stellar • Talk Shows on Mute • Wish You Were Here.

VOL. 41 – ERIC CLAPTON   00699669 / $14.95
After Midnight • Can't Find My Way Home • Forever Man • I Shot the Sheriff • I'm Tore Down • Pretending • Running on Faith • Tears in Heaven.

VOL. 42 – CHART HITS   00699670 / $14.95
Are You Gonna Be My Girl • Heaven • Here Without You • I Believe in a Thing Called Love • Just Like You • Last Train Home • This Love • Until the Day I Die.

VOL. 43 – LYNYRD SKYNYRD   00699681 / $14.95
Don't Ask Me No Questions • Free Bird • Gimme Three Steps • I Know a Little • Saturday Night Special • Sweet Home Alabama • That Smell • You Got That Right.

VOL. 44 – JAZZ   00699689 / $14.95
I Remember You • I'll Remember April • Impressions • In a Mellow Tone • Moonlight in Vermont • On a Slow Boat to China • Things Ain't What They Used to Be • Yesterdays.

VOL. 46 – MAINSTREAM ROCK   00699722 / $14.95
Just a Girl • Keep Away • Kryptonite • Lightning Crashes • 1979 • One Step Closer • Scar Tissue • Torn.

VOL. 47 – HENDRIX SMASH HITS   00699723 / $16.95
All Along the Watchtower • Can You See Me? • Crosstown Traffic • Fire • Foxey Lady • Hey Joe • Manic Depression • Purple Haze • Red House • Remember • Stone Free • The Wind Cries Mary.

VOL. 48 – AEROSMITH CLASSICS   00699724 / $14.95
Back in the Saddle • Draw the Line • Dream On • Last Child • Mama Kin • Same Old Song & Dance • Sweet Emotion • Walk This Way.

VOL. 50 – NÜ METAL   00699726 / $14.95
Duality • Here to Stay • In the End • Judith • Nookie • So Cold • Toxicity • Whatever.

VOL. 51 – ALTERNATIVE '90S   00699727 / $14.95
Alive • Cherub Rock • Come As You Are • Give It Away • Jane Says • No Excuses • No Rain • Santeria.

VOL. 56 – FOO FIGHTERS   00699749 / $14.95
All My Life • Best of You • DOA • I'll Stick Around • Learn to Fly • Monkey Wrench • My Hero • This Is a Call.

VOL. 57 – SYSTEM OF A DOWN   00699751 / $14.95
Aerials • B.Y.O.B. • Chop Suey! • Innervision • Question! • Spiders • Sugar • Toxicity.

Prices, contents, and availability subject to change without notice.

FOR MORE INFORMATION, SEE YOUR LOCAL MUSIC DEALER,
OR WRITE TO:

HAL•LEONARD®
CORPORATION

7777 W. BLUEMOUND RD. P.O. BOX 13819 MILWAUKEE, WI 53213

Visit Hal Leonard online at www.halleonard.com

0106

GUITAR BIBLES

from 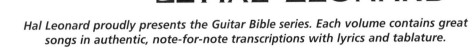 HAL•LEONARD®

Hal Leonard proudly presents the Guitar Bible series. Each volume contains great songs in authentic, note-for-note transcriptions with lyrics and tablature.

ACOUSTIC GUITAR BIBLE
35 acoustic classics: Angie • Building a Mystery • Change the World • Dust in the Wind • Hold My Hand • Iris • Maggie May • Southern Cross • Tears in Heaven • Wild World • and more.
00690432...$19.95

ACOUSTIC ROCK GUITAR BIBLE
35 classics: And I Love Her • Behind Blue Eyes • Come to My Window • Free Fallin' • Give a Little Bit • More Than Words • Night Moves • Pink Houses • Slide • 3 AM • and more.
00690625...$19.95

BABY BOOMER'S GUITAR BIBLE
35 songs: Angie • Can't Buy Me Love • Happy Together • Hey Jude • Imagine • Laughing • Longer • My Girl • New Kid in Town • Rebel, Rebel • Wild Thing • and more.
00690412...$19.95

BLUES GUITAR BIBLE
35 blues tunes: Boom Boom • Hide Away • I Can't Quit You Baby • I'm Your Hoochie Coochie Man • Killing Floor • Pride and Joy • Sweet Little Angel • The Thrill Is Gone • and more.
00690437...$19.95

BLUES-ROCK GUITAR BIBLE
35 songs: Cross Road Blues (Crossroads) • Hide Away • The House Is Rockin' • Love Struck Baby • Move It On Over • Piece of My Heart • Statesboro Blues • You Shook Me • more.
00690450...$19.95

CLASSIC ROCK GUITAR BIBLE
33 essential rock songs: Beast of Burden • Cat Scratch Fever • Double Vision • Free Ride • Hard to Handle • Life in the Fast Lane • The Stroke • Won't Get Fooled Again • and more.
00690662...$19.95

COUNTRY GUITAR BIBLE
35 country classics: Ain't Goin' Down • Blue Eyes Crying in the Rain • Boot Scootin' Boogie • Friends in Low Places • I'm So Lonesome I Could Cry • T-R-O-U-B-L-E • and more.
00690465...$19.95

DISCO GUITAR BIBLE
30 stand-out songs from the disco days: Brick House • Disco Inferno • Funkytown • Get Down Tonight • I Love the Night Life • Le Freak • Stayin' Alive • Y.M.C.A. • and more.
00690627...$17.95

EARLY ROCK GUITAR BIBLE
35 fantastic classics: Blue Suede Shoes • Do Wah Diddy Diddy • Hang On Sloopy • I'm a Believer • Louie, Louie • Oh, Pretty Woman • Surfin' U.S.A. • Twist and Shout • and more.
00690680...$17.95

FOLK-ROCK GUITAR BIBLE
35 songs: At Seventeen • Blackbird • Fire and Rain • Happy Together • Leaving on a Jet Plane • Our House • Time in a Bottle • Turn! Turn! Turn! • You've Got a Friend • more.
00690464...$19.95

GRUNGE GUITAR BIBLE
30 songs: All Apologies • Counting Blue Cars • Glycerine • Jesus Christ Pose • Lithium • Man in the Box • Nearly Lost You • Smells like Teen Spirit • This Is a Call • Violet • and more.
00690649...$17.95

HARD ROCK GUITAR BIBLE
35 songs: Ballroom Blitz • Bang a Gong • Barracuda • Living After Midnight • Rock You like a Hurricane • School's Out • Welcome to the Jungle • You Give Love a Bad Name • more.
00690453...$19.95

INSTRUMENTAL GUITAR BIBLE
37 great instrumentals: Always with Me, Always with You • Green Onions • Hide Away • Jessica • Linus and Lucy • Perfidia • Satch Boogie • Tequila • Walk Don't Run • and more.
00690514...$19.95

JAZZ GUITAR BIBLE
31 songs: Body and Soul • In a Sentimental Mood • My Funny Valentine • Nuages • Satin Doll • So What • Star Dust • Take Five • Tangerine • Yardbird Suite • and more.
00690466...$19.95

MODERN ROCK GUITAR BIBLE
26 rock favorites: Aerials (System of a Down) • Alive (P.O.D.) • Cold Hard Bitch (Jet) • Kryptonite (3 Doors Down) • Like a Stone (Audioslave) • Whatever (Godsmack) • and more.
00690724...$19.95

NÜ METAL GUITAR BIBLE
25 edgy metal hits: Aenema • Black • Edgecrusher • Last Resort • People of the Sun • Schism • Southtown • Take a Look Around • Toxicity • Youth of the Nation • and more.
00690569...$19.95

POP/ROCK GUITAR BIBLE
35 pop hits: Change the World • Heartache Tonight • Money for Nothing • Mony, Mony • Pink Houses • Smooth • Summer of '69 • 3 AM • What I Like About You • and more.
00690517...$19.95

R&B GUITAR BIBLE
35 R&B classics: Brick House • Fire • I Got You (I Feel Good) • Love Rollercoaster • Shining Star • Sir Duke • Super Freak • and more.
00690452...$19.95

ROCK GUITAR BIBLE
33 songs: All Day and All of the Night • Born to Be Wild • Day Tripper • Hey Joe • Jailhouse Rock • Money • Paranoid • Sultans of Swing • Walk This Way • You Really Got Me • more!
00690313...$19.95

ROCKABILLY GUITAR BIBLE
31 songs from artists such as Elvis, Buddy Holly and the Brian Setzer Orchestra: Blue Suede Shoes • Hello Mary Lou • Peggy Sue • Rock This Town • Travelin' Man • and more.
00690570...$19.95

SOUL GUITAR BIBLE
33 songs: Groovin' • I've Been Loving You Too Long • Let's Get It On • My Girl • Respect • Theme from Shaft • Soul Man • and more.
00690506...$19.95

SOUTHERN ROCK GUITAR BIBLE
25 southern rock classics: Can't You See • Free Bird • Hold On Loosely • La Grange • Midnight Rider • Sweet Home Alabama • and more.
00690723...$19.95

Prices, contents, and availability subject to change without notice.

FOR MORE INFORMATION, SEE YOUR LOCAL MUSIC DEALER, OR WRITE TO:

HAL•LEONARD®
CORPORATION
7777 W. BLUEMOUND RD. P.O. BOX 13819 MILWAUKEE, WI 53213

Visit Hal Leonard online at **www.halleonard.com**

0606

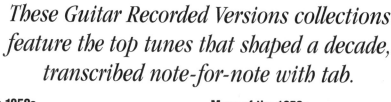